MMA Mastery
Strike Combinations

Mark Hatmaker

MMA Mastery
Strike Combinations

Mark Hatmaker

MMA Mastery #3

Cover photo by Mitch Thomas
Interior photos by Doug Werner

Tracks Publishing
San Diego, California

MMA Mastery
Strike Combinations
Mark Hatmaker

Tracks Publishing
140 Brightwood Avenue
Chula Vista, CA 91910
619-476-7125
tracks@cox.net
www.startupsports.com
trackspublishing.com

Copyright © 2011 by Doug Werner and Mark Hatmaker
10 9 8 7 6 5 4 3 2 1

Publisher's Cataloging-in-Publication
Hatmaker, Mark.

    MMA mastery: strike combinations / Mark Hatmaker ; cover photo by Mitch Thomas ; interior photos by Doug Werner. -- San Diego, Calif. : Tracks Pub., c2011.

        p. ; cm.
        (MMA mastery ; #3)

        ISBN: 978-1-935937-22-7
        Includes index.

        1. Mixed martial arts--Training. 2. Hand-to-hand fighting--Training. 3. Martial arts--Striking. 4. Wrestling--Training. 5. Self-defense--Training. I. Werner, Doug, 1950- II. Title. III. Title: Strike combinations. IV. Title: Mixed martial arts mastery: strike combinations. V. Series: MMA mastery ; no. 3.

GV1102.7.M59 H383 2011   2011924369
796.815--dc22   1106

Books by Mark Hatmaker

No Holds Barred Fighting:
The Ultimate Guide to Submission Wrestling

More No Holds Barred Fighting:
Killer Submissions

No Holds Barred Fighting:
Savage Strikes

No Holds Barred Fighting:
Takedowns

No Holds Barred Fighting:
The Clinch

No Holds Barred Fighting:
The Ultimate Guide to Conditioning

No Holds Barred Fighting:
The Kicking Bible

No Holds Barred Fighting:
The Book of Essential Submissions

Boxing Mastery

No Second Chance:
A Reality-Based Guide to Self-Defense

MMA Mastery:
Flow Chain Drilling and Integrated O/D Training

MMA Mastery:
Ground and Pound

Books are available through major bookstores
and booksellers on the Internet.

Acknowledgements
Phyllis Carter
Kylie Hatmaker
Dan Marx
Jackie Smith
Mitch Thomas
Shane Tucker

Warning label
The fighting arts include contact and can be dangerous. Use proper equipment and train safely. Practice with restraint and respect for your partners. Drill for fun, fitness and to improve skills. Do not fight with the intent to do harm.

Contents

How to Use the MMA Mastery and NHBF Manuals

This book and the others in this series are meant to be used in an interlocking, synergistic manner where the sum value of the manuals is greater than the individual parts. What we are striving to do with each manual is to focus on a specific aspect of MMA and give thoughtful consideration to the necessary ideas, tactics and strategies pertinent to the facet of focus. We are aware that this piece-

meal approach may seem lacking if one consumes only one or two manuals at most, but we are confident that once three or more manuals have been studied the overall picture or method will begin to reveal itself.

Since the manuals are interlocking there is no single manual in the series that is meant to be complete in and of itself. Instead, we think of each manual as an individual piece or section of a comprehensive master manual (with this volume, the master manual clocks in at over 2,900 pages). For example, although *NHBF: Savage Strikes* is a thorough compendium on MMA/self-defense striking, it is bolstered with side-by-side study of *Boxing Mastery*. While the book *NHBF: Killer Submissions* introduces the idea of chaining submissions and can be used as a solitary tool, it is made all the stronger by an understanding of the material that preceded it in the first submission manual, *NHBF: The Ultimate Guide to Submission Wrestling.*

And so on and so forth with each manual in this series. With that out of the way, Let's talk combinations.

Introduction
Punches in Bunches

Never having shot is always to have missed.
— Dutch Proverb

Throw enough dirt and some will stick.
— 17th Century Proverb

One of the identifying earmarks of the novice (or unthinking) fighter is the tendency to throw strikes in isolation.

Punches in bunches ... Combinations ... Hit 'em hard, hit 'em often ... These phrases and many others are used to express the wisdom of striking in multiples as opposed to looking for the one punch knockout (aka the Sunday Punch). One of the identifying earmarks of the novice (or unthinking) fighter is the tendency to throw strikes in isolation — a jab here, a low kick there, here an overhand, there a looping haymaker, everywhere a waste of energy.

Single strikes allow your opponent to respond with single defensive measures in a one-to-one ratio. This tit-for-tat form of fighting is simplistic, predictable and easily upset by introducing complexity. And the easiest way to introduce complexity into the offensive equation is not to come up with some esoteric strike, but to throw more strikes. Not more as in the throwing 80 jabs in a round, but more as in throwing at least one other strike after each jab (three total is ideal). More on that in a bit.

Defense is a responsive reaction by definition. To defend there must be an offense preceding. No offense, no need for defense. Simple enough, right? We must keep in mind that any responsive action (as defense is) is always (always!) slower than offense. All offensive actions are the first out of the gate. Defensive reactions cue off the offensive start and must play catch up in an attempt to thwart the offense.

> The easiest way to introduce complexity into the offensive equation is not to come up with some esoteric strike, but to throw more strikes.

In addition to the late starting nature of the defensive reaction, we must also contend with the entropy induced by "guesstimation." Even the best defenders are making guesses as to what exact strike is coming his or her way. What angle, velocity and power might be behind it. He must determine whether or not the action is indeed a strike or a feint. You couple the late start of reacting to an action with the entropy of cognitive guesstimation and we see that action (offense) always has odds over reaction (defense).

The reactive nature of defense is a slow pony versus

> Combinations work so well at adding complexity because human beings are horrible multi-taskers.

offense. It is for this reason that good shell position (defensive posture) is wiser than parrying or cuffing strategies and the like. Yes, these strategies can work, but simply covering vulnerable targets with a good defensive posture is a better bet when we put offense and defense in race terms. Even with the odds stacked in favor of offense in a one-to-one ratio (one strike versus one defensive reaction), we can increase the odds for the striker and reduce the defender's reactive speed simply by starting more horses out of the gate.

Combinations work so well at adding complexity because human beings are horrible multi-taskers.

Subtract Multi-tasking

We human beings are mighty fortunate. There are countless tools available that allow us to get more done faster. Each month the iPhone adds more apps to make life easier, computers improve performance exponentially and other fruits of technology seem to keep apace. These technological increases are often due to improvements in the dual arenas of memory and parallel processing. These tools are a boon to human productivity because they are capable of performing many tasks, often at the same time, that we mortals either cannot do on our own or don't have the time to do.

We build these awesome machines that perform so well, all the while being painfully aware that we, ourselves, cannot perform these tasks very well at all.

The bad news (well, bad if you don't accept the limits of your own brain) is that we do not have an expandable memory interface or efficient parallel processing. What I mean is that our memory, as seemingly prodigious as it is, only works when we "work with it." We can't simply observe and/or practice a good jab, kick, choke or joint lock once or twice and expect it to be there when we call it up as you might the directions to a restaurant with an iPhone app.

Our memory is of the kind that needs maintenance and reinforcement to make information actually stick. It is for this reason that we should pick and choose our input wisely.

Our memory is of the kind that needs maintenance and reinforcement to make information actually stick. It is for this reason that we should pick and choose our input wisely. Human memory improvement is so time consuming that we should opt for efficient, effective memories as opposed to storing any old thing that comes down the pike. We can adapt the computer axiom of Garbage In, Garbage Out —GIGO — and replace that phrase with — Genius In, Genius Out — and seek the best information to fill the hard drive in our heads.

Most of us are all too familiar with the shortcomings of our own memories, but we often forget to include the shortcomings of our task processing systems. These days the cheapest of laptops can truly multi-task. They can surf the Web with more than a few viewing windows open at once, stream music from iTunes and keep track of your word document all at the same time (as is occurring at the writing of this sentence). This awesome multi-tasking capability is the result of parallel processing — a system that allows multiple tasks to be performed simultaneously. We humans simply aren't built that way. We are not parallel processors but serial processors who trick ourselves into thinking we are multi-tasking when we aren't.

Take this example. You are driving and your favorite tune is blaring. You come to a busy intersection where you must wait for an opportune time to cross traffic. Researchers have found that when humans are placed in this exact situation, most turn down the music until they have traversed the intersection. Why should this be? You don't need your eyes to hear music. You don't need your ears to scan the traffic for the best moment to cross. Experiments with many different scenarios of human multi-tasking find the same results. Humans who are "multi-tasking" are actually making rapid shifts in attention back and forth between the tasks they are currently engaged in — and doing neither one particularly well. Just think about the last time you tried to talk with someone who was surfing the Internet, texting or reading while claiming to be paying attention to your conversation. How well were they listening?

Computers and other parallel processors don't do this performance shifting. As I key in this sentence my music doesn't stop streaming, the Web browser doesn't stall — all continue to operate beautifully. But I, the lowly serial processing human, must pay attention to this sentence before I can really hear what tune is playing (one of Green Day's newest).

Now, let's take this serial versus parallel processing to the fight game. The most efficient manifestation of physical movement will be rapid serial processing as opposed to simultaneous action. This means that we should trim all offensive/defensive tools down to their bare minimum and insure that we perform one task and then the next and then the next and so on. We should dump simultaneous strikes (elbows accompanied by a foot stomp, for example) not just because they are mechanically unsound, but because study after study shows us that human beings do best with single tasks as opposed to multiple ones. Keep in mind that this advice is for simultaneous movement and not for serial strategies. You can box to set up your takedown (an excellent strategy, by the way), but boxing while hitting your takedown is inadvisable.

Wise combat arts coaches, whether aware of the human serial processing research or not, have long echoed this 1-2-3 approach. Boxing coaches urge their fighters to "stick and move" (jab and then move) not "stick while moving." Knowledgeable grappling coaches exhort their students to "wrestle for position before submission" as opposed to fishing for the submission before position has been attained. In the area of street self-defense, Tony Blauer sagely pronounced in

> In light of the best research into how the human mind works, we would be wise to skip texting while driving, forgo reading our Kindles while talking with our families and eschew throwing a jab while hitting a double leg.

regard to fighting multiple attackers, "You don't fight five guys at the same time, you fight five guys one at a time."

In light of the best research into how the human mind works, we would be wise to skip texting while driving, forgo reading our Kindles while talking with our families and eschew throwing a jab while hitting a double leg. Because our serial processing minds make erratic shifts in attention to mimic parallel processing, we wind up doing none of these tasks well. In the fight, as in life, let's stick with the basics, one thing at a time — stick and move. Our performances will be better for it.

Let's take this to our subject of focus — combinations. Combinations are wisely devised as a series of sequential strikes with zero parallel overlap occurring. By taking the initiative in combination striking and focusing on each strike in the series, we can strengthen our game — this much is a given. But in order to exploit the serial processing nature of our opponents' minds, again, combinations are the answer. By striking, you place your opponent in a position of defensive

The fight metrics conducted specifically for this volume show, overwhelmingly, that it is the third strike in the combination that finds its target.

reaction. For him to return fire, he must switch continually between an offensive and defensive mindset. And as we have seen in other realms of human performance, it is often during this switch that the onslaught catches up to a mistimed processing switch, and the combination does the trick.

With all this good news about the power of combinations, it might be reasonable to assume the more strikes, the better, right? Maybe not.

The Numbers

We came to the conclusions in this material using fight metrics, a statistical training tool introduced in a previous volume in this series. (For more on fight metrics and how to apply statistical analysis to fight training, see our volume in this series *NHBF: The Essential Book of Submissions*.)

We sampled numerous professional MMA fights for this volume, 535 of them to be exact, all sampled from elite level competition — UFC, PFC and WEC. Of the 535 fights, the majority were won via strikes (confirming the hypothesis of the 640 fight sample used in *NHBF: The Essential Book of Submissions*). Of the sampled 535 fights, approximately 80 percent of them featured good combination work. Any fight that seemed to feature primarily single shots (the occasional jab or leg kick) was tossed so that we could focus on fights (and fighters) who use combination work. We wanted to find out what does, indeed, work in practice and not merely in theory.

Now, let's have a look at a seemingly magic number.

Power of 3's: Part One

We humans love our threes. It's always "three guys walk into a bar" never four or five. It's the Three Stooges even though there were six total. And for many the best ménage is a trois. Outside of these loose examples (three of them, by the way) three is the optimal number of strikes in an MMA combination. Throw one strike and you have no combination, throw two and you haven't approached enough escalated complexity to bollix up your opponent. The fight metrics conducted specifically for this volume show, overwhelmingly, that it is the third strike in the combination that finds its target.

Our observations find that single strikes (the jab, by far the most common) used as probes, disrupters and distance finders land approximately 40 percent of the time. When a second shot was fired, making this a two-point combination, the second shot landed approximately 43 percent of the time. Now there's not much difference between 40 percent for strike one and 43 percent for strike two. There is a slight uptick in landing the second shot, but not enough to base a two strike per combination strategy on. It's when we get to the third strike where things get interesting.

The third strike in a three-point combination landed somewhere near 66 percent of the time. Whether this whopping increase in landing is due to the increased complexity of defense we discussed earlier or some other factor I can't say. But the exponential escalation of landing success is inarguable (at least in the fights sampled).

So strike one and strike two have approximately the same odds of landing success. But there seems to be something about strike numero tres that has mojo written all over it. Whether that mojo is deteriorating defensive capacity in the face of complexity or whatever factor, the odds say getting to strike three is mighty wise.

If three is good, four has got to be better, right? Again, maybe not.

Power of 3's: Part Two

When combinations made it as far as the fourth or fifth strike, there was a precipitous drop in landing success. Strike four drops to 49 percent (even odds ain't bad), but strike five hits a low of 38 percent. Why?

The answer(s), and this is mere supposition, might be threefold (how's that for holding a theme?).

Once the defending fighter is struck, his or her body often lurches in ways not predictably readable in the standard defensive vocabulary sense. This may cause the offensive fighter to miss as the struck fighter provides "air."

Firing a combination anything above three seems to inspire a change in mode. With that in mind, it might be wise to advise a three strikes and you're out (or in) mindset — fire your three and move out or in to clinch or shoot.

Or it could be that the offending fighter, finding some "bite" with his strikes, may become a bit overzealous and start winging the strikes following the bite. It's easy to envision this rush to success sometimes getting in the way of precision.

Or the answer could lie in the nature of the sport itself. MMA is not boxing. MMA is not kickboxing. And MMA is not Muay Thai. An obvious observation, but one that may go a long way toward explaining the drop off. In any of the aforementioned sports, combination landing success can reach higher than three, but these sports have less complexity to deal with. MMA fighters also have the clinch, the takedown and even standing submission attempts to deal with. As striking pressure increases, the defending fighter will often seek to switch mode (clinching, shoot a takedown). This could very well be the root of the magic number three observation. Firing a combination with more than three strikes seems to inspire a change in mode. With that in mind, it might be wise to advise a three strikes and you're out (or in) mindset — fire your three and move out or in to clinch or shoot.

> When one of your strikes finds some major bite (odds are it's number three) and you've got your opponent reeling, it is time to swarm.

Whether the answer is found in the above guesses, I cannot say. But the statistical data makes a strong case for beating 50/50 odds of landing by making three-point combinations your default striking strategy. Throwing less or more may be a waste of energy (keep in mind that probes/jabs are never a waste). In a sport with such maximum expenditures of energy, it might be wise to play odds and conserve energy where we can and burst where the numbers dictate.

With that said, this book is based on the power of 3's with one exception …

Power of 3's: Part Three

The exception? Finishing. When one of your strikes finds some major bite (odds are it's number three) and you've got your opponent reeling, it is time to swarm. Feel free to climb your strike numbers higher than three to get the job done. But if you are a numbers oriented, empirical evidence based fighter — and if he's not reeling — it's three strikes and you're out.

Where Does Punching Power Come From?

Pop Quiz! No worries, there's only one question and it's a multiple choice format.

Question: Where do strikes get their power?

A. Arms for punches and legs for kicks.
B. Hips.
C. From the ground up (i.e, the feet).
D. From the core.
E. All of the above.

If you answered E, pat yourself on the back. If you answered anything else, well, you are still partially correct.

There is a tendency for some to compartmentalize the body saying that power resides in this or that particular aspect. But truth be told, the human body works as a single cohesive unit to throw powerful strikes.

We need all of the aforementioned factors (plus timing, of course).

Those convinced that it is only a single factor should try the following experiments.

Experiment One
Work a tough boxing round on the heavy bag while on your knees and see how hard you hit without generating power from your feet.

Experiment Two
Stand with your back to a low wall, pressing your buttocks firmly against it. Have a partner take you through a focus pad round without you taking either butt cheek off of the wall and see how powerful you feel without your hips in play.

Experiment Three
Throw on a body protector and lace it tight. Fill any gaps between you and the body protector with anything to reduce core/torso mobility (rags, T-shirts). Once you feel appropriately immobilized, bang the bag for a round. That feel as strong as usual?

The body uses the feet, the legs, the hips, the core, the shoulders, the arms and the ineffable attribute of timing to bring power to strikes. With that in mind, we can assume that any striking approach that seeks to limit "your source of power" to one or two focus points is poorly thought out. The body can fire shots utilizing only a few of the mentioned tandem aspects, but chances are those shots carry nowhere near the power potential they could. When a fighter is criticized for "arm punching," it means he's using only the strength of the arms or shoulders, thus mitigating power potential. Don't be that fighter.

The Power of Counter Revolution
One way to ensure that you bring more body into your

strikes is to strive for counter revolution in your striking. Counter revolution, by its very definition, demands that you reverse the momentum/direction of the body dictated by the previously fired shot. This means you bring the body back into maximum alignment to power the next strike. So how do we harness this power of counter revolution? That's easy — strike from alternate sides of the body.

> Counter revolution, by its very definition, demands that you reverse the momentum/direction of the body dictated by the previously fired shot. This means you bring the body back into maximum alignment to power the next strike.

Let's play this out to bring the point home. Stand up right now (assuming you are seated) and throw a jab. Assuming the jab was thrown properly, did you feel how the lead hip and shoulder advance with the punch? How your body pivots toward your inside (toward your chest) over the lead foot? Good. Now throw a cross (or rear kick, or rear hook or any other shot from the opposite side of your body — no spinning shots). Notice how your rear hip and shoulder advance with this opposite side shot and advance the entire body as well? That is counter revolution.

> Every good boxing, kickboxing and Muay Thai coach knows that the difference between good fighters and great fighters is footwork.

Let's stay on our feet for another moment. Throw that jab again. Now throw a second punch with that same arm or a kick off of the same side leg. With the body already advanced toward your lead side because of the jab, the second shot has very little "body advance" to add to its power. Whatever power there is must come from perhaps only two or three body parts (say arms/shoulders and a tiny bit of core whip).

To make the preceding experiments all the more convincing, go to the heavy bag and bang for a round using counter revolution and then bang for a round using only strikes off a single side of the body. Assess for both speed and power, and I'll wager that you'll see what I mean.

Don't get me wrong, firing the occasional strike from the same side can have its advantages …

Advantage One
Surprise. Once you've set a rhythm of counter revolution combinations, an occasional same side combination can punctuate your offense and upset your opponent's defensive rhythm.

Advantage Two
Speed. Doubling up (particularly with punches) can be faster than counter revolution. The doubling or even tripling up on same side combinations may not necessarily have stopping/dropping power, but simply landing strikes may create that psychological entropy that allows you to garner more success with your counter revolution striking.

Smart Feet, Smart Fighter (Lazy Style)

Every good boxing, kickboxing and Muay Thai coach knows that the difference between good fighters and great fighters is footwork. Most all instruction in striking arts begins with footwork. Yet it seems this is the lesson most often forgotten or completely skipped to get to the "good stuff" (actually, it might be a tie between footwork and keeping your hands up).

I hear lip service to the power of footwork and then ignoring the practice of footwork because striking is where it's at. It's fun to bang the bag, strike the pads and score on a sparring partner, and not nearly as viscerally rewarding to shuffle, sidestep and pivot. Strikes are the bang, the punctuation that ends fights in easy demonstrable fashion. Mario Yamasaki has never raised a fighter's hand while Bruce Buffer intoned, "Winner by way of good lateral movement!" Yeah, there's no way to make footwork dramatic. Yet it is absolutely key.

Muhammad Ali in his prime or Anderson Silva at the top of his game were masters of slippery footwork, but these elusive artists were often booed in the midst of these demonstrations of "now he's here, now he's gone" ability. The fans want KOs. The judges give more weight to successful offense than to successful defense, and for these reasons (among others) we have lots of pressure to devalue what we claim to prize so greatly.

Good fighters can hit; great fighters can hit and move. Good fighters can bang and wade right in. Great fighters can get inside, bang away and then be gone. Good fighters try to tag the other guy while great fighters stick and move. If you prefer analogies, think of your strikes as artillery — you may have superior fire-power in both hands, both feet, both elbows and both knees, but without artillery transport to get that high-powered ordnance into firing range, there ain't no fight happening.

We covered footwork in detail in two previous manuals, *NHBF: Savage Strikes* and *Boxing Mastery*. If you'd like some detailed instruction regarding the topic, check out those manuals. What I will do here is pare down that footwork material and remove foot-work as an isolated lesson altogether. We will apply a stripped down footwork vocabulary that is integrated directly into every drill in this manual. By making foot-work a part of each combination, we build elusive mobility directly into our training and stop giving lip service to an integral aspect of the game.

I recommend that you work each combination round at an absolute minimum of three rounds. I will assume that you are using the industry standard of five-minute rounds.

You can work the trinity of footwork approaches whether you are shadow striking, doing mirror work, banging the bag, using focus pads or doing live fire drills with a partner. Assuming, again, that you work this a bare minimum of three rounds, I suggest you work them in the following manner.

Round One: In & Out

Step in to fire your combination and then leave immediately. To enter simply ...
1. Drive off the rear foot.
2. Step the lead foot toward your target.
3. Attempt to time the landing of the first shot with the landing of the lead foot.
4. Once the combination has been fired ...
5. Drive off the lead foot toward the rear.
6. Step with the rear foot — holding your guard throughout.

Round Two: Outside Lateral Movement

Here you are sidestepping toward your lead side. Keep in mind you can combine In & Out with either Lateral Movement drill to close range, but the purpose of this drill is to keep it simple — simply to develop movement. Lateral Movement is ideal versus an advancing fighter — you do not want to be the fighter who retreats in a linear fashion. Your retreating strikes will have little (if any) bang to them. Retreating linear motion is ideal for power strikers, clinch artists and shooters to capitalize upon.

To move laterally to the outside ...

1. Step your lead foot toward the same side of the body (orthodox fighters will step their lead foot/left foot to the left and southpaws vice versa).
2. As soon as the lead foot lands, pivot on the ball of the lead foot swinging your rear foot toward the outside (left or right, respectively according to stance leads).
3. You will now be facing your advancing opponent — fire your combination.

Note

In an ideal world you will always move laterally away from your opponent's power side, which is usually his rear side. When facing an orthodox stance, you want to move toward your right/his left. Facing a southpaw, move to his right/your left. You may adjust if you have more respect for the fighter's lead hook than his rear hand.

Round Three: Inside Lateral Movement

The mirror of the preceding round.
1. Step the rear foot toward the same side (orthodox stances will step their rear right foot toward their right and southpaws vice versa).
2. As soon as the rear foot lands, pivot on the ball of the foot and wheel your stance to face your advancing opponent.

If you look at the aforementioned volumes regarding footwork, you will see that we subdivide footwork into eight directions. But I think you will find this trinity of movement (particularly when made part of the striking drill set) will serve the purpose of making you far more elusive in both your offense and defense. If you decide not to integrate these three movement drills, I urge you to move in some fashion while striking.

Please do not get stuck in a rut of standing stock still in front of the bag or your focus pad feeder and banging away. This sort of static banging holds very little transfer to the fight and may be counterproductive. I also urge you to not get locked into the fencer's dilemma of assuming only linear motion — move back, move forward. The rules of fencing dictate such

You may have superior firepower in both hands, both feet, both elbows and both knees, but without artillery transport to get that high-powered ordnance into firing range, there ain't no fight happening.

motion, but MMA is not locked into such an easy-to-read dichotomy. By cutting movement from eight directions to three, doesn't make it elementary work. This power of three is more than enough to smarten your feet and your fighting.

Head Kicks? Nope

Spoiler alert. The combinations within will feature punches, leg and body kicks, knees and elbows but, as you've already read, zero head kicks. The nutshell rationalization for this exclusion is twofold.

Head kicking is energy intensive (and we're talking energy intensive in what is already an energy consuming sport). There are plenty other weapons of choice that do just as much damage with less effort.

The head kick has a 50/50 "Ooops!" rate. That means 50 percent of the time the fighter throwing the kick either slips to the canvas (effectively taking himself down) or spins and turns his back with a miss providing a nice entry for the opponent. No other offensive gambit provides this dire an outcome (although hip and arm throws come close). For more details on the numbers and the empirical justification of the head kick exclusion, see our previous volume in this series, *NHBF: The Book of Essential Submissions*.

If you dearly relish head kicks, have Clay Guida bundles of energy to burn and are comfortable with the 50/50 chance of landing on your butt, you can take any combination that features a body kick and substitute a head kick. I recommend that you make the substitution only with body kicks and not leg kicks because the set ups are often predicated differently.

> In a nutshell, you miss waaayyy more than you hit.

I Miss You

One of the most illuminating stats in boxing is the punch count. That bit of data that tells you how many punches each fighter has thrown each round and how many punches have landed. This info is available for MMA post-fight, but as of this writing has not been included as part of the between round analysis in televised bouts (here's to that changing soon since it's mighty useful info). The most interesting thing about those numbers is the ratio between punches thrown and punches landed. In a nutshell, you miss waaayyy more than you hit.

Let's wrap our heads around this. Professionally trained boxers, whose job is to punch people, punch air more than they punch people. Even the best of the best, the champions and the ranked up-and-comers may land more than their opponents, but they all miss more punches than they land. And guess what? When it comes to MMA, the ratio is a little wider. Elite level MMA competitors and challengers alike miss more than they hit. I'm not just talking missed punches, but missed kicks, missed knees, missed elbows and failed shots. And we've all seen the disappointing loss of a seemingly airtight submission attempt (and many, many not so airtight sub attempts).

> The most under-used, underutilized, undervalued weapon is the almighty jab.

So, what's the lesson here? Do these fighters just suck? Of course not. The lesson is that the target in front of them is also an elite athlete whose job is not to be hit. An obvious observation, but we need to factor in the disparity between missing and landing in our training. We often tout "How you train is how you'll fight" and to a large degree this is true. But we must also inform this training with the corollary maxim of "Let your training be reflective of the battlefield."

Combine the two maxims and you have a simple two pronged plan for your training approach. But we must admit that an often overlooked aspect of training is taking into account the wide miss margin. Missing eats energy, sometimes more energy than landing a shot. Missing pulls you out of position. Missing leaves you vulnerable to counters. We must prepare for this inevitable miss rate. But how?

Shadowboxing and bag work can't do it. Missing "on purpose" is not really missing because you the thinker will always be the originator of the thought "I'll miss this shot now" and then adjust your power, balance and recoil accordingly. No, to train for missing (and you will miss) you must actually miss. And that's where a good focus pad/Thai pad feeder comes into play.

I've already offered the suggestion of a minimum of three five-minute rounds per combination so that you can work the trinity of footwork. But I find it has been quite useful to add at least one additional round of banging the pads in which your feeder randomly removes a pad element or two to get you used to that "Shit! Where did that go?" feeling.

Don't start out the miss work on the first round. It's nice to bite the pads for a few rounds so that you learn to cultivate your power, timing, recoil and speed. A good feeder will recognize when you've found your groove and provide that bit of chaos. I think you'll find adding the chaos of missing into your pad feeding is yet another intelligent rung in reflecting the actual conditions inside the ring or cage.

Again, you'll miss more than you'll hit during a fight, so you might as well get a taste of it in your training.

Your Super, Not So Secret Weapon

The most underused, underutilized, undervalued weapon is the almighty jab. Yeah, you've heard all of this before, but stay with me for another page and hear it again.

The jab is the king of punches. You wanna start a combination with your quickest and most direct weapon?

The jab's your man. You wanna set up a kick or a knee or an elbow, who you gonna call on? The jab again. Wanna set up a takedown with an offensive probe that both distracts and let's you know if your opponent is in range? The jab. Need to interrupt your opponent's offensive rhythm? Jab. Need to get on your bicycle to shake off a heavy shot while still appearing active to the judges? Jab. Need an energy conserving probe to see what your opponent's reactions are like? Jab. Need the fastest weapon in your arsenal that is both an offensive and defensive tool? The jab.

The jab is the highest yielding tool in both boxing and MMA (for those who use it, that is). The jab is, probably, all the more useful in MMA as it sets up and/or foils so many varied offensive gambits.

The second reason it's more useful to the MMA athlete is glove size.

The 4-6 ounce glove sizes in MMA as opposed to the 12-16 ounce range in boxing gloves means MMA gloves, at their largest, are still 50 percent lighter than their smallest counterpart in boxing. This means greater havoc can be delivered with both hands with less effort. The jab, in boxing, can be merely bothersome as opposed to injurious. In MMA the lighter gloves allow a minority of jabs to build up some eye-closing damage. Witness the effective jab work of Dan Hardy, Terry Etim or B.J. Penn, for example.

The jab is your #1 BFF. Use it to probe, gauge and evaluate the combinations to best be used against your opponent.

The jab is the highest yielding tool in both boxing and MMA (for those who use it, that is). The jab is, probably, all the more useful in MMA as it sets up and/or foils so many varied offensive gambits.

Menus

We are finally at the physical instruction portion of this material. We have subdivided the combinations into a variety of categories so that you can easily locate the combinations pertinent to your situational needs.

We first divide the combinations into two- and three-point combinations, meaning two strikes are thrown per combination in two-point combinations, and three strikes are thrown in three-point combinations. Yes, I know I harped on throwing only in three's. I advise novices to start with the two-point combinations working with the body mechanics of multi-firing until they are comfortable with the tools that comprise them and then move to the three-point combinations. Those with intermediate skills can jump to the statistically preferred three pointers.

We also subdivide according to the tools that comprise the combinations with punches being the common denominator for most all combinations. By subdividing the tools, those who favor knees can easily locate the menus featuring knees; a fighter who needs to brush up on boxing and elbows can flip to that section; a fighter who wishes to emulate BJ Penn's striking prowess and throw perhaps only one or two leg kicks in his entire career can avoid the kicking menus altogether. And so on.

I'll mention the protocol one more time and assume that the protocol will be observed throughout — a minimum of three rounds per combination. Four, if you have a feeder to give you misses.

1. Punch Combinations
Two-Point Combos

Double jab head

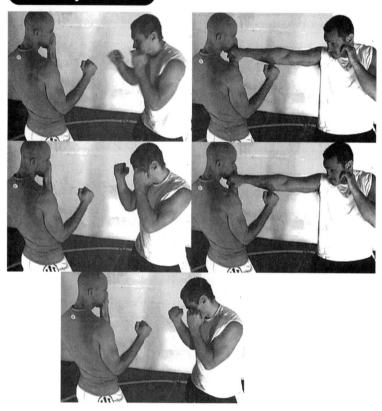

Jab head / jab body

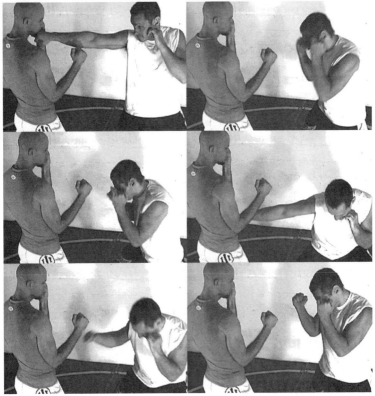

● Anytime you finish with a low punch, you must retreat low. Do not stand up to full height until you are out of countering range.

Jab body / jab head

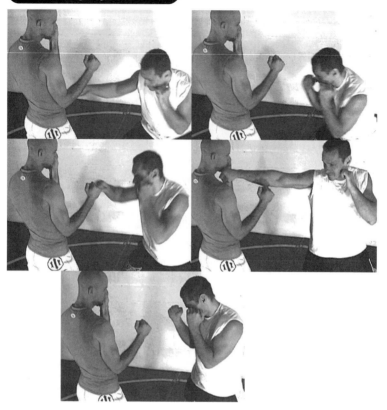

Double jab body

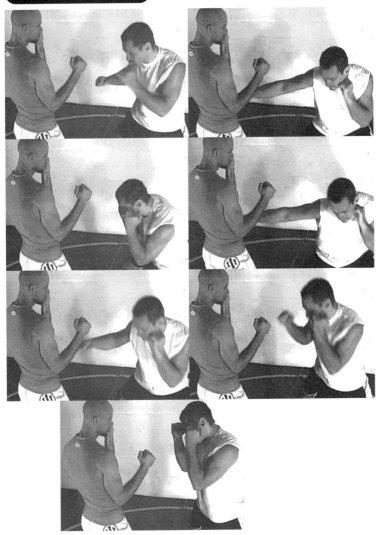

Jab head / Cross head

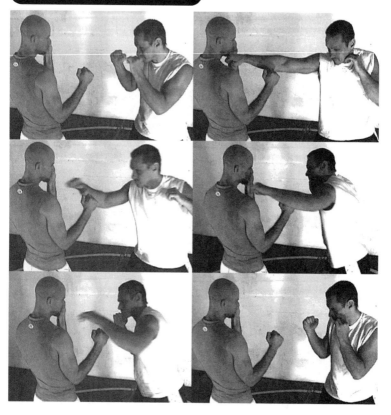

Jab head / Cross body

Jab body / Cross head

Jab body / Cross body

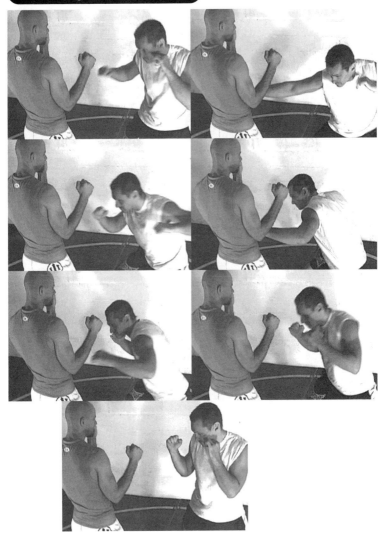

Jab head / Lead hook head

Jab body / Lead hook head

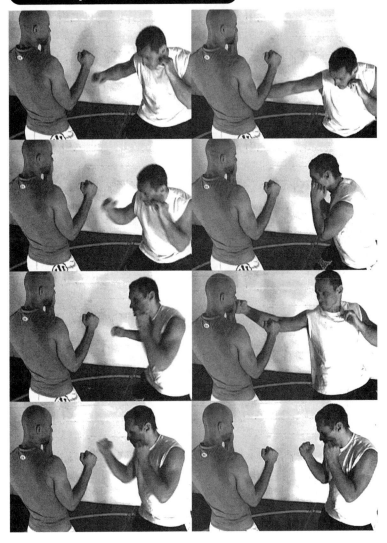

Jab body / Rear hook head

Jab head / Lead uppercut

Jab head / Rear uppercut

Jab head / Rear hook head

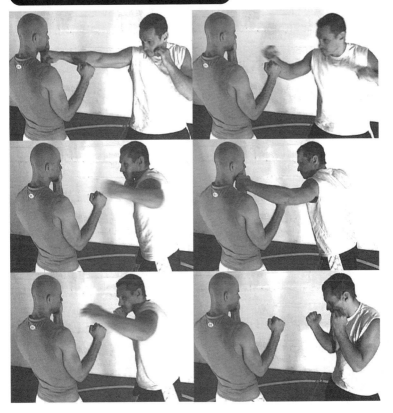

Lead uppercut / jab head

Cross head / Lead hook head

Cross body / Lead hook head

Cross head / Lead hook body

Double lead hooks, low to high

To double up on a hook, fire the first hook to the body. Then cock the firing hand 45 degrees and down approximately 6 to 8 inches to gain some loading power. Then fire to the head.

Double rear hooks, low to high

Lead hook head / Lead uppercut

Lead hook head / Cross body

Lead uppercut / Rear hook head

Lead uppercut / Rear uppercut

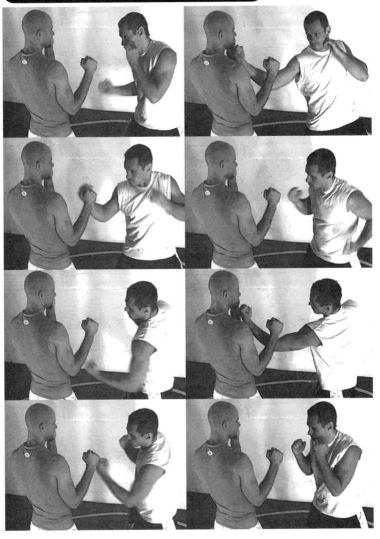

Rear uppercut / Lead hook head

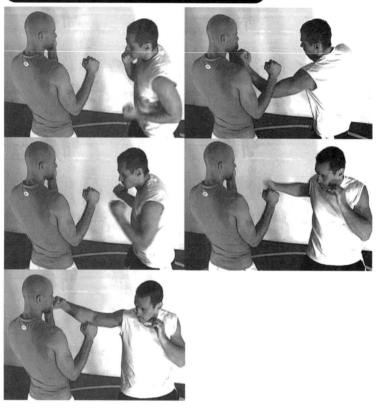

Rear uppercut / Cross head

Rear uppercut / Jab

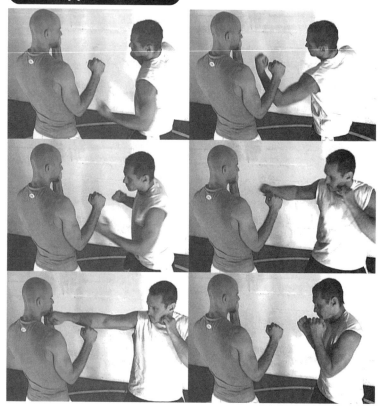

Lead hook head / Rear hook head

Lead hook head / Rear uppercut

Rear hook head / Rear uppercut

Rear uppercut / Rear hook head

Lead hook head / Spinning hammerfist

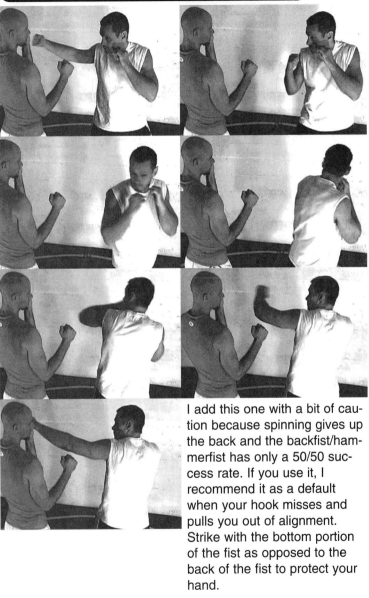

I add this one with a bit of caution because spinning gives up the back and the backfist/hammerfist has only a 50/50 success rate. If you use it, I recommend it as a default when your hook misses and pulls you out of alignment. Strike with the bottom portion of the fist as opposed to the back of the fist to protect your hand.

2. Punch Combinations
Three-Point Combos

Triple jab head

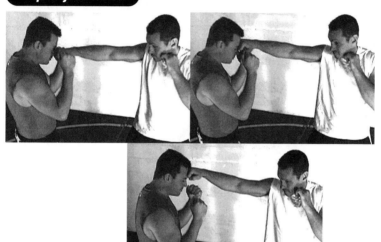

Jab head / Lead hook head / Lead uppercut

Jab head / Lead uppercut / Lead hook head

Jab head / Jab head / Cross head

Jab head / Jab body / Rear hook head

Jab head / Cross head / Lead hook head

Jab head / Cross head / Lead hook body

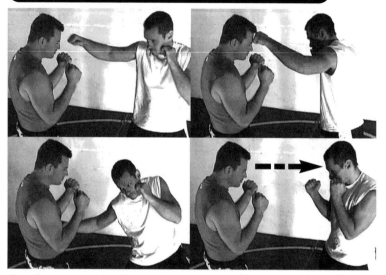

Anytime a combination ends on a low punch, you must either clinch or exit immediately or you will find yourself open for counters.

Jab head / Cross head / Lead uppercut

Jab head / Lead hook head / Rear hook head

Jab head / Lead hook head / Rear uppercut

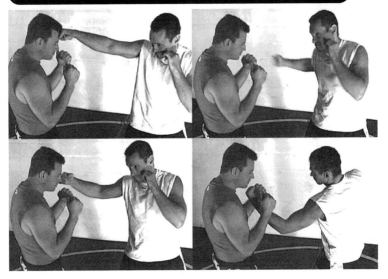

Jab head / Overhand / Lead shovel hook

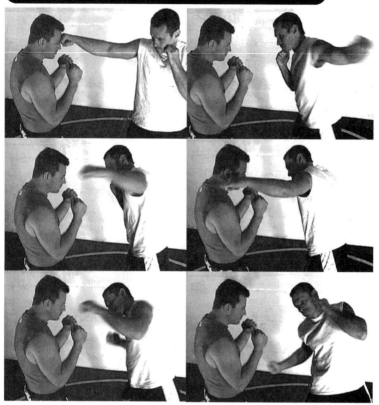

Cross head / Lead hook head / Cross head

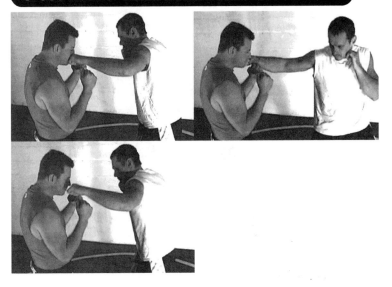

Lead hook head / Cross head / Lead hook head

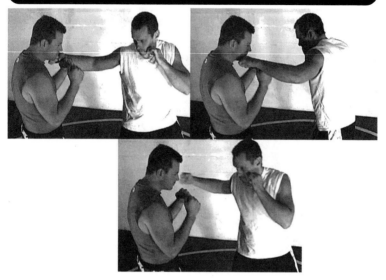

Lead hook head / Lead uppercut / Cross head

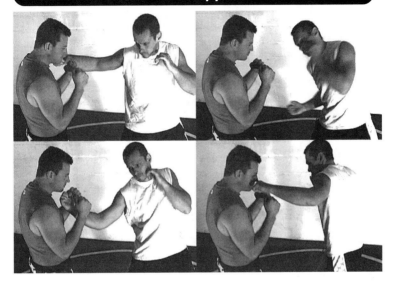

Lead hook head / Lead uppercut / Rear hook head

Lead hook body / Lead hook head / Rear uppercut

Jab head / Cross body / Lead hook head

Jab head / Cross head / Jab head

Jab head / Cross head / Cross head

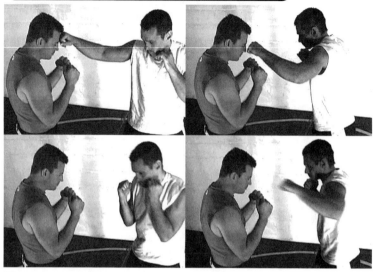

There is a brief lull between the two crosses as you reload. While not as strong as counter revolution or speedy as double jabbing, this combo has its uses.

Jab head / Rear uppercut / Lead hook head

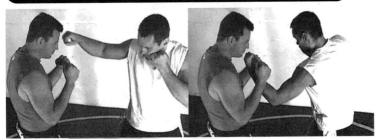

Jab head / Lead hook head / Cross head

Jab head / Lead hook head / Rear uppercut

Jab / Lead hook body / Lead hook head

Jab / Lead uppercut / Rear hook head

Lead uppercut / Rear hook head / Lead hook head

3. Punch and Kick Combinations
Two-Point Combos

Jab head / Leg kick

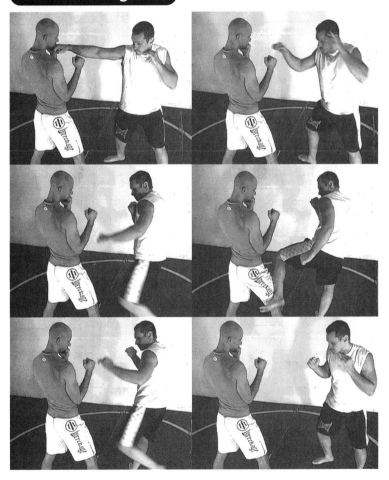

Jab head / Body kick

Jab head / Inside kick

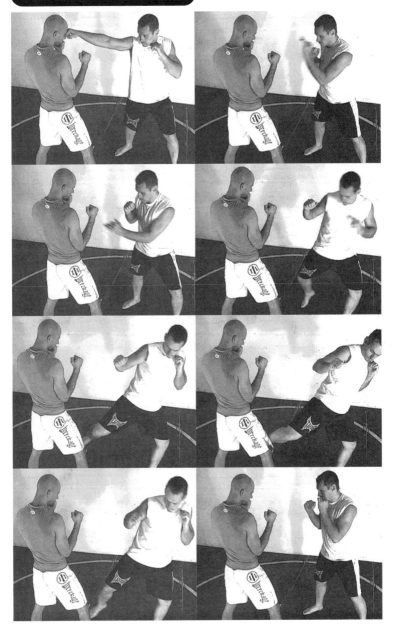

Jab head / Switch kick leg

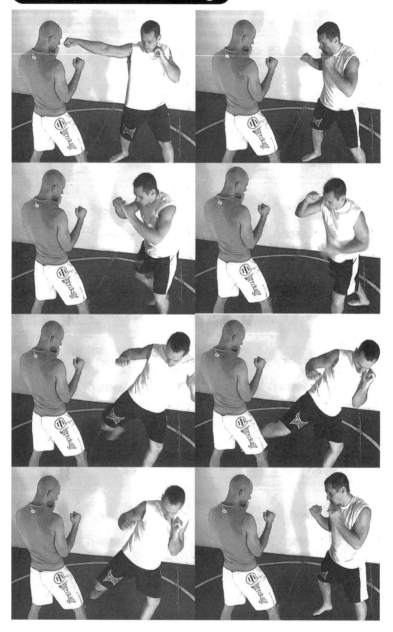

Jab head / Switch kick body

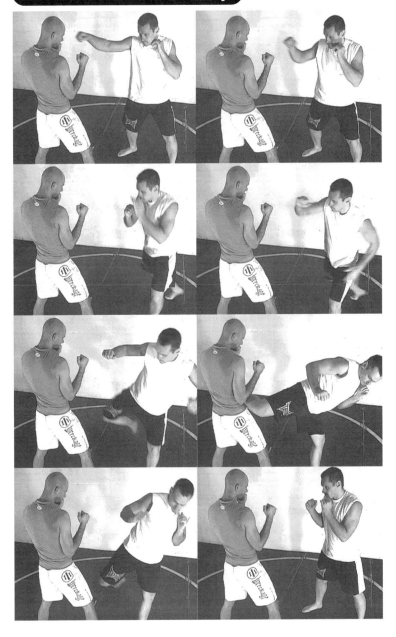

Jab head / Spinning back kick

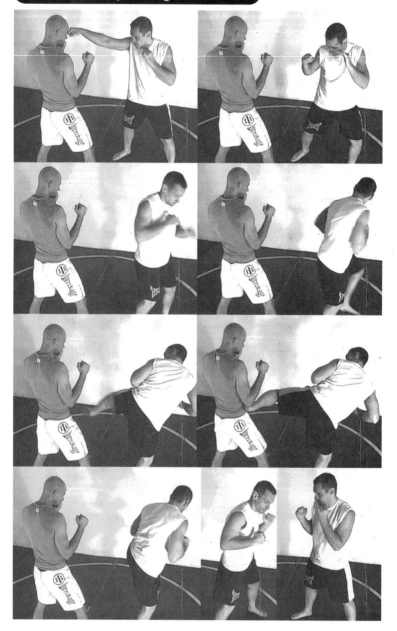

Cross head / Switch kick leg

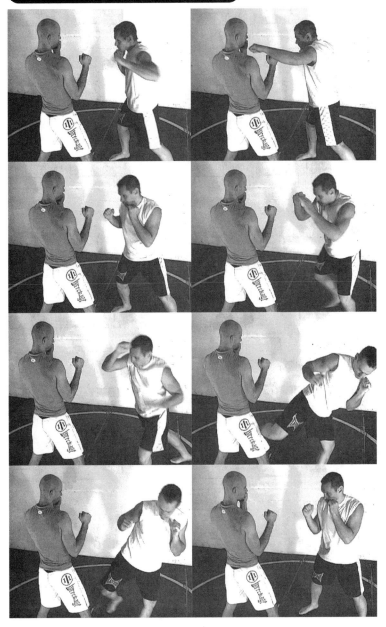

Cross head / Switch kick body

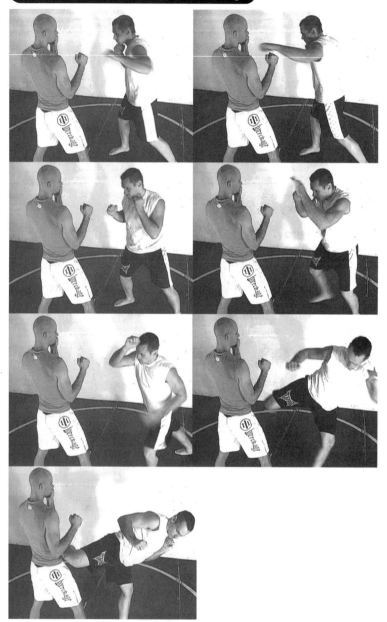

Lead hook head / Leg kick

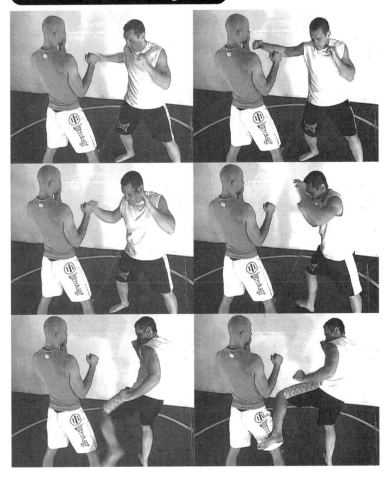

Lead hook head / Body kick

Rear hook head / Leg kick

Jab kick / Cross head

Cross kick / Jab head

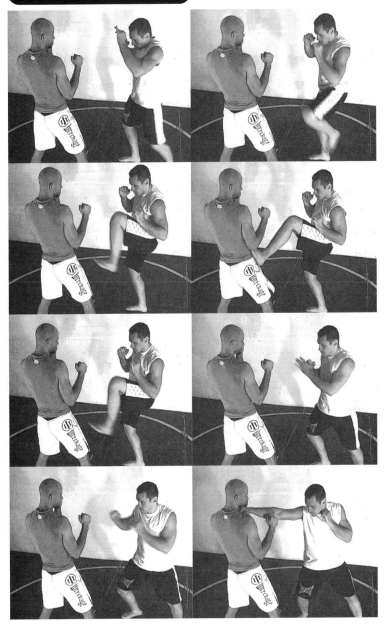

Cross kick / Lead hook head

Lead uppercut / Leg kick

Lead uppercut / Body kick

Rear uppercut / Switch kick leg

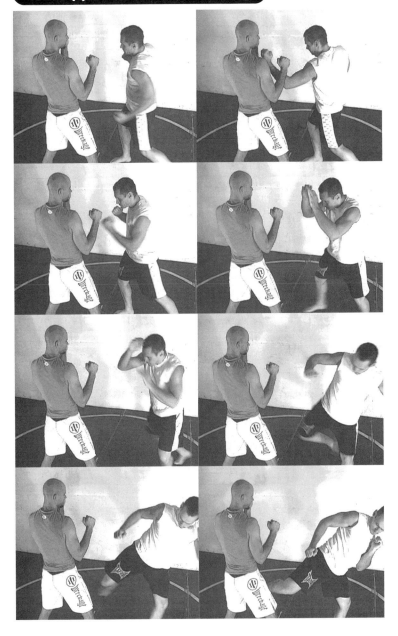

Rear uppercut / Switch kick body

Lead side kick / Jab head

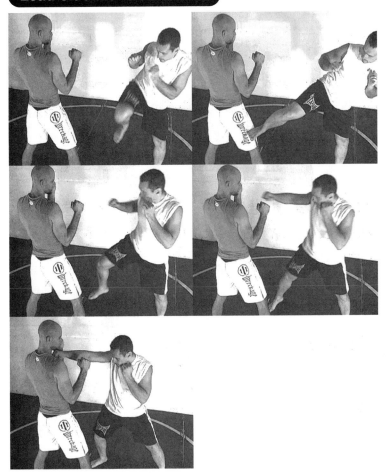

Switch cross / Leg kick

To switch cross, execute the foot work for a switch kick and time the rear hand (now in the lead) to land as soon as the new lead foot hits the mat. From this new lead, fire the rear kick.

4. Punch and Kick Combinations
Three-Point Combos

Jab head / Cross head / Switch kick leg

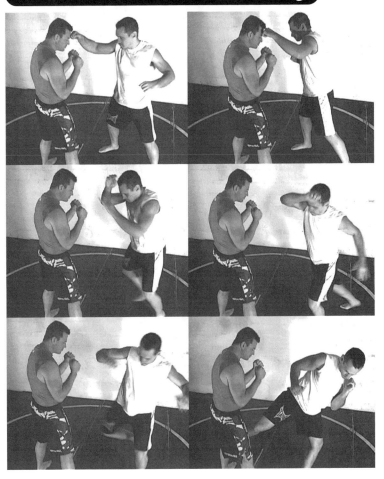

Jab head / Cross head / Switch kick body

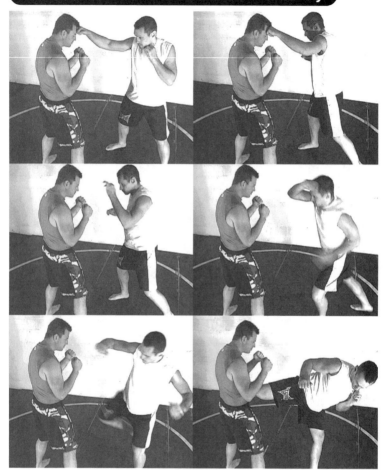

Jab head / Cross head / Leg kick

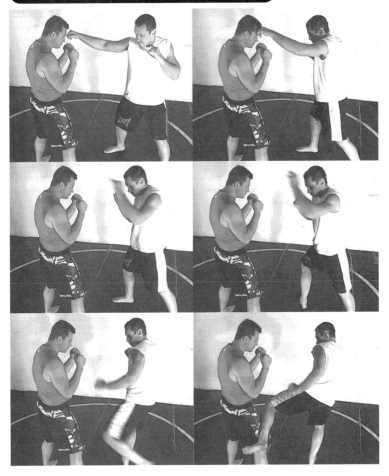

Jab head / Cross head / Body kick

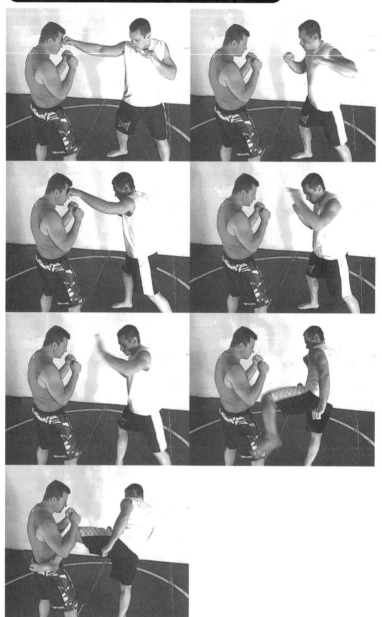

Jab head / Cross head / Inside kick

Jab head / Inside kick / Cross head

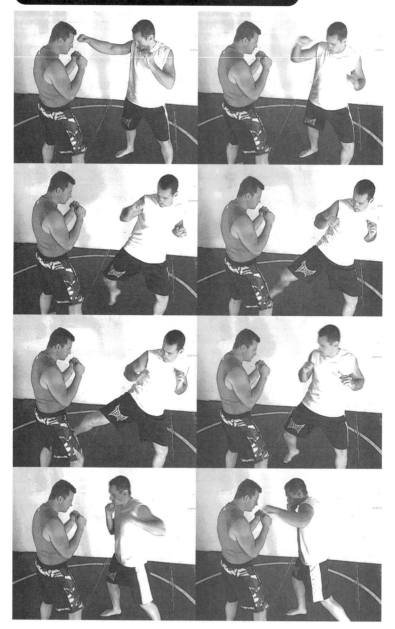

Jab head / Jab kick / Jab head

Jab head / Switch kick leg / Rear uppercut

Jab kick / Cross head / Lead hook head

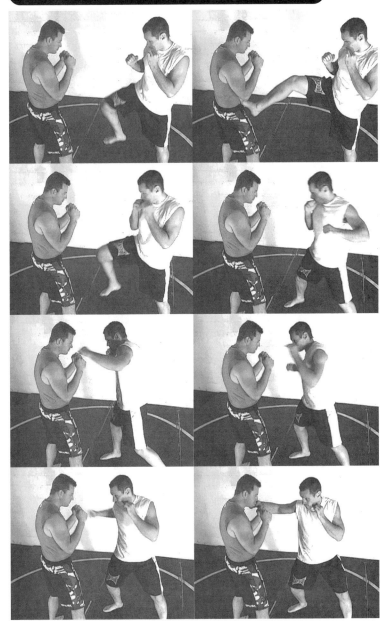

Jab kick / Lead hook head / Cross head

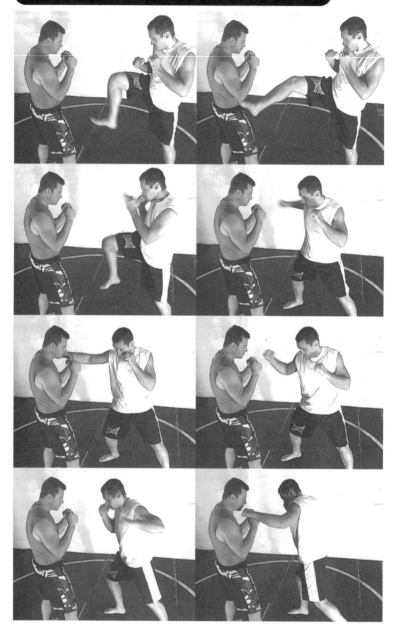

Jab head / Side step / Leg kick

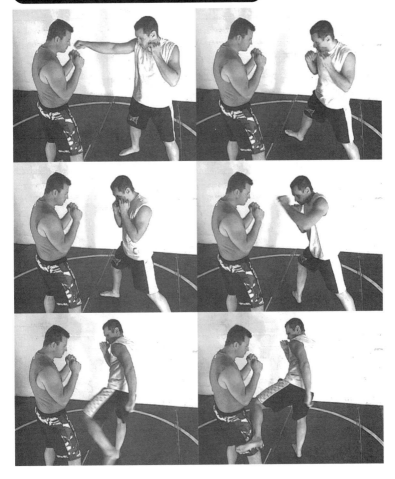

Cross head / Lead hook head / Leg or body kick

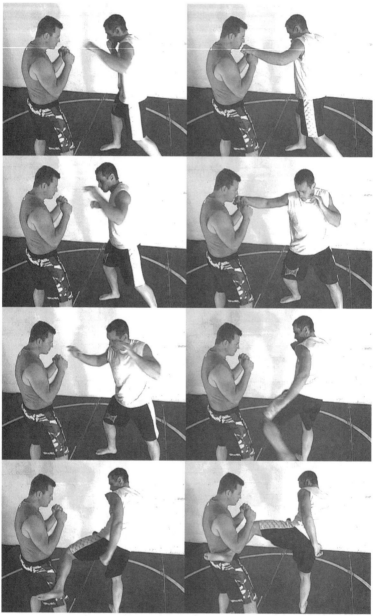

Finish with a leg or body kick.

Cross head / Lead hook head / Inside kick

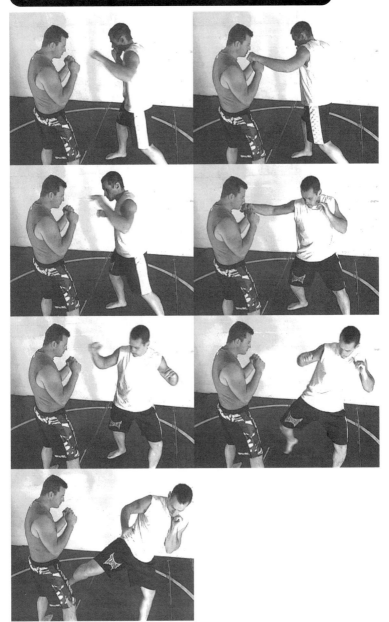

Cross head / Jab head / Inside kick

Cross head / Jab head / Cross kick

Cross head / Body kick / Cross head

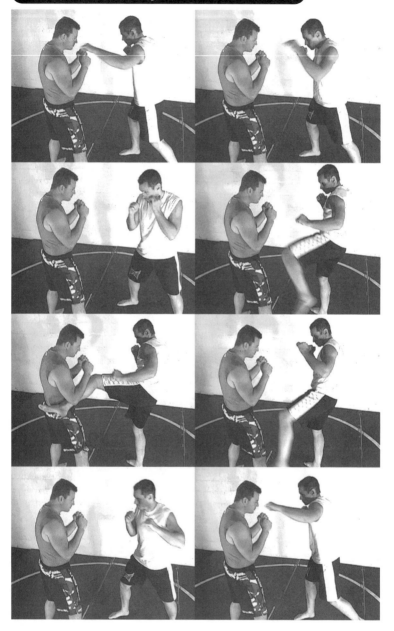

Lead hook head / Cross head / Switch kick leg or body

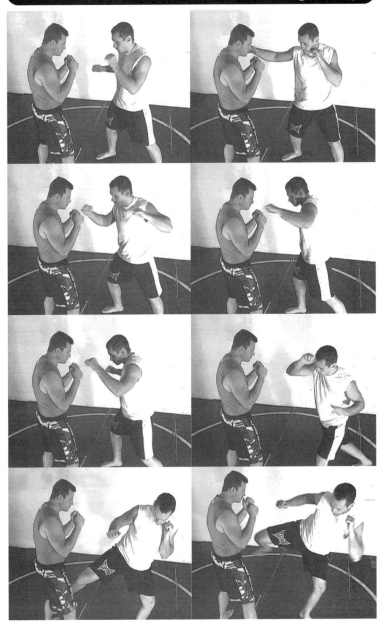

Finish with a switch kick leg or body.

Leg kick / Cross head / Lead hook head

Body kick / Cross head / Lead hook head

Jab kick / Cross head / Lead hook head

Cross kick / Lead hook head / Cross head

Lead uppercut / Cross head / Switch kick leg

Lead uppercut / Cross head / Switch kick body

Jab head / Rear uppercut / Switch kick leg

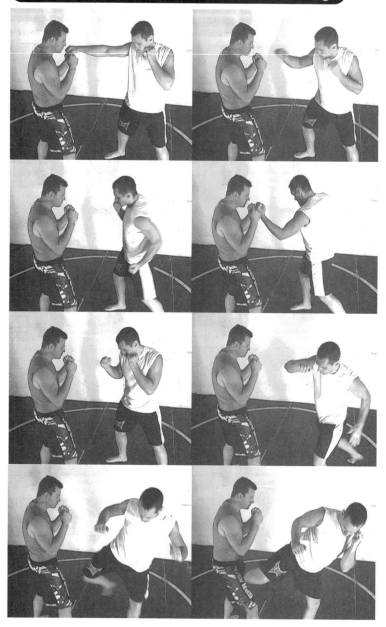

Jab head / Rear uppercut / Switch kick body

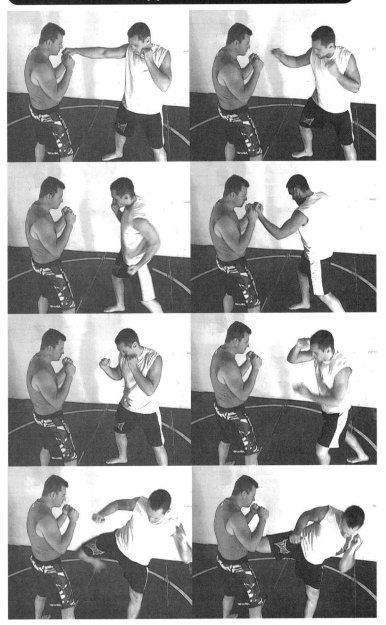

Cross head / Lead uppercut / Leg or body kick

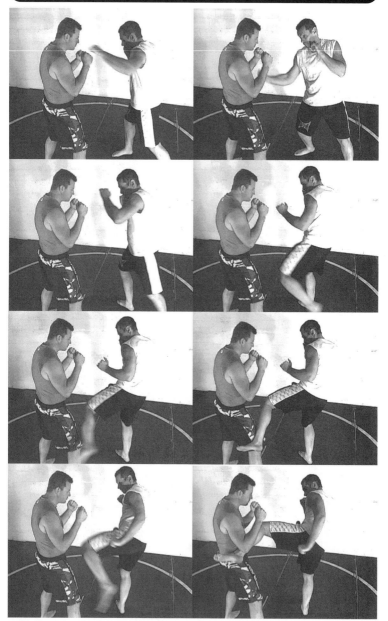

Finish with a leg or body kick.

Inside kick / Cross head / Lead hook head

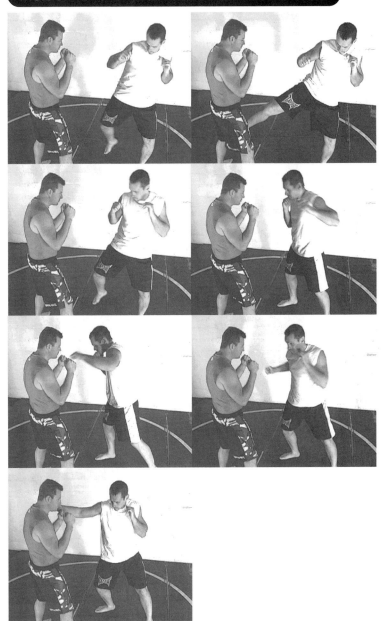

Side kick / Jab head / Cross head

Rear kick / Cross head / Lead hook head

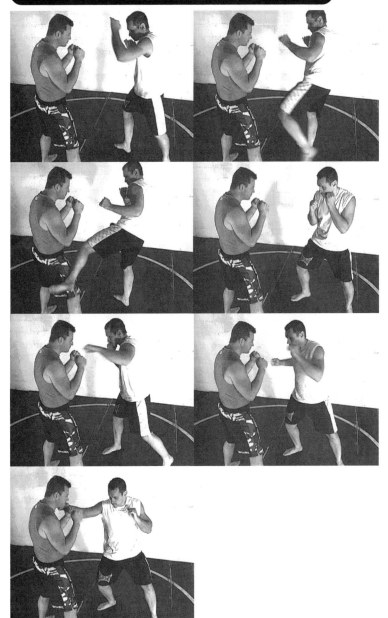

Jab head / Feint cross / Switch kick leg

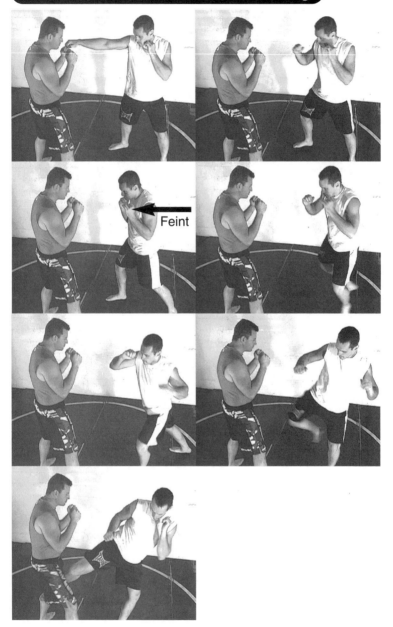

Feint

Jab head / Feint cross / Switch kick body

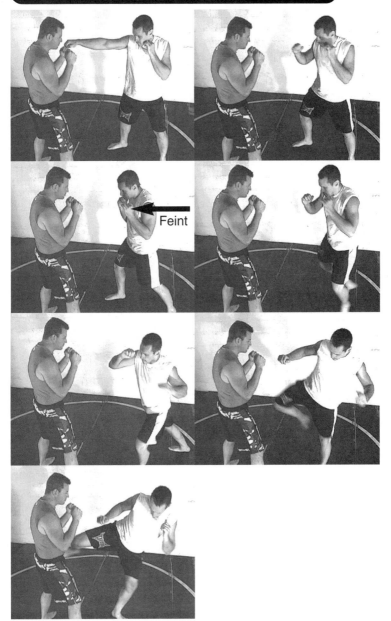

Feint

Jab head / Feint rear kick / Switch kick leg or body

Finish with a switch kick leg or body.

Jab head / Feint rear kick / Leg or body kick

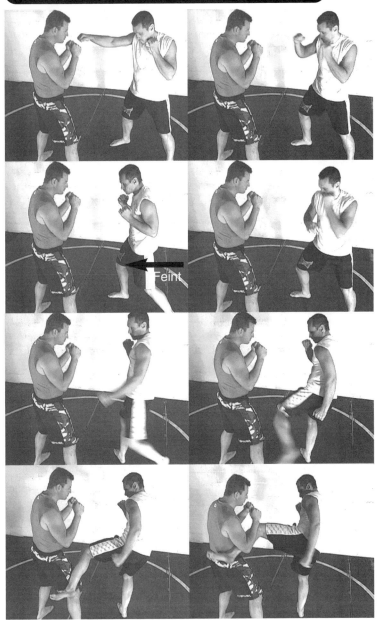

Finish with a leg or body kick.

5. Elbow Combinations
Two-Point Combos

Lead elbow / Rear elbow

Up elbow / Rear elbow

Lead hook head / Spinning elbow

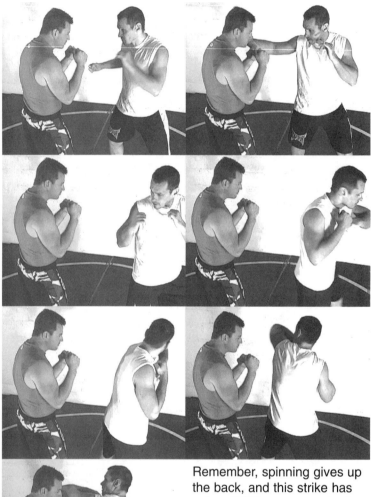

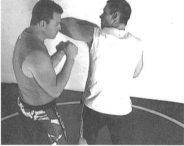

Remember, spinning gives up the back, and this strike has only a 50/50 success rate. I recommend it as a default when your hook misses and pulls you out of alignment.

6. Punch and Elbow Combinations
Two-Point Combos

Jab head / Cross elbow

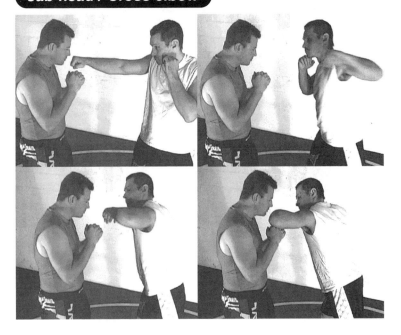

Cross head / Lead elbow

Cross body / Lead up elbow

Lead hook head / Rear elbow

Jab head / Lead elbow

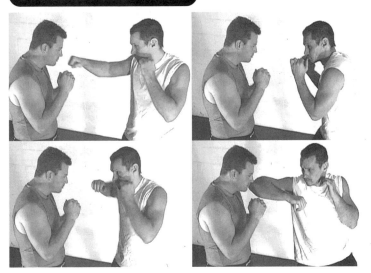

7. Punch and Elbow Combinations
Three-Point Combos

Jab head / Cross head / Lead elbow

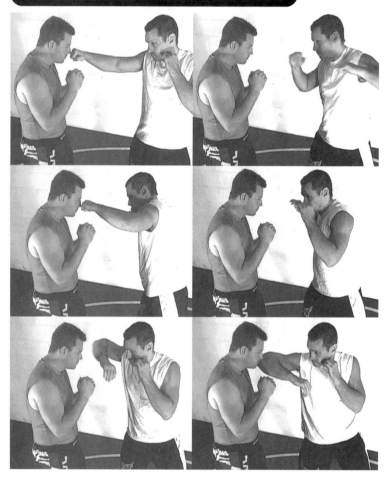

Jab head / Lead elbow / Rear elbow

Cross head / Lead hook head / Cross elbow

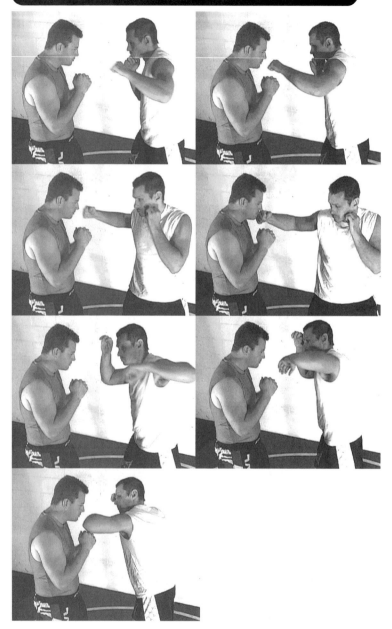

Cross head / Rear elbow / Cross head

Jab head / Cross head / Lead up elbow

Cross head / Lead up elbow / Rear elbow

Rear uppercut / Lead hook head / Rear elbow

Cross head / Lead hook body / Rear elbow

Lead hook body / Rear elbow / Lead up elbow

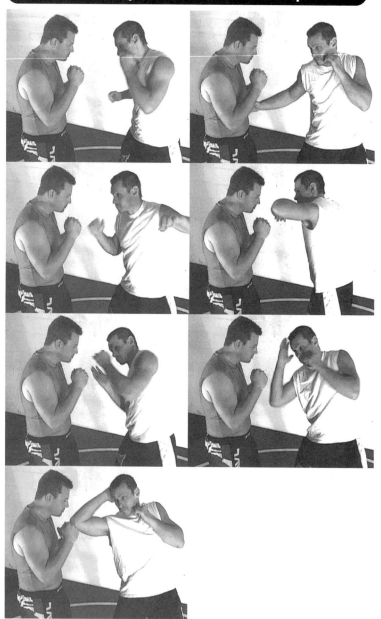

8. Knee Combinations

Lead straight knee / Rear straight knee

Thai clinch / Rear skip knee / Spin

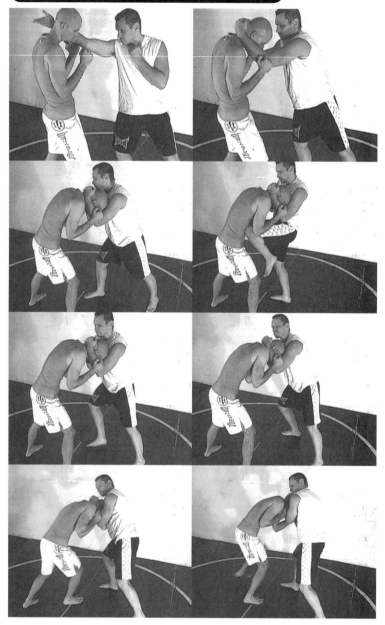

Thai clinch / Rear skip knee / Lead skip knee / Spin

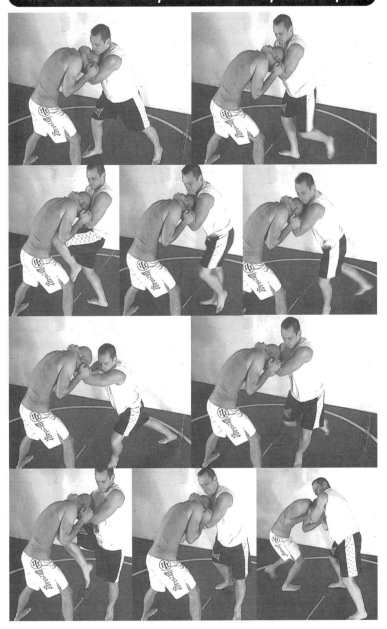

9. Punch and Knee Combinations

Two-Point Combos

Jab head / Rear knee

Cross head / Lead skip knee

Lead hook head / Rear knee

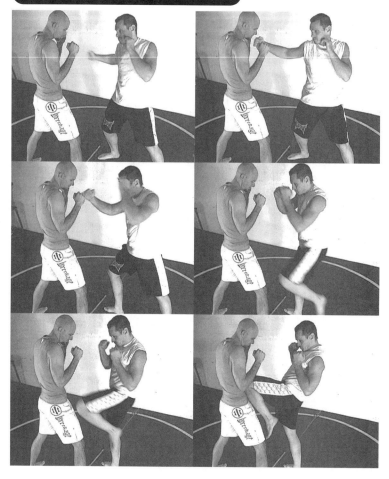

10. Punch and Knee Combinations
Three-Point Combos

Jab head / Cross head / Lead skip knee

Jab or cross head / Clinch / Rear knee

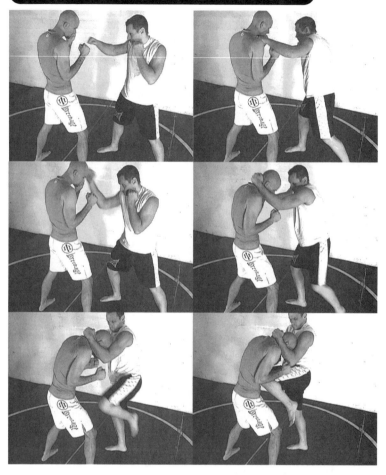

Lead hook head / Rear uppercut / Rear knee

Overhand / Head control / Lead skip knee

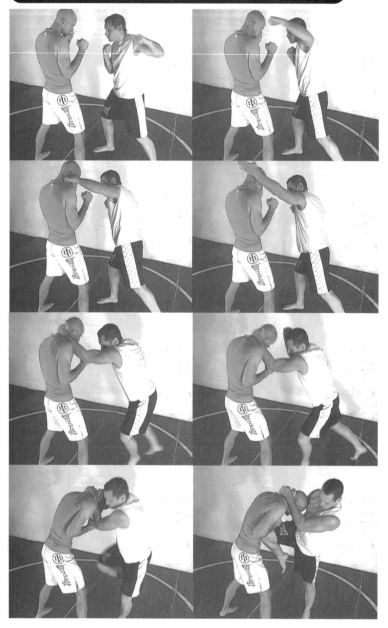

11. Elbow and Knee Combination
Three-Point Combo

Up elbow / Cross elbow / Clinch / Rear knee

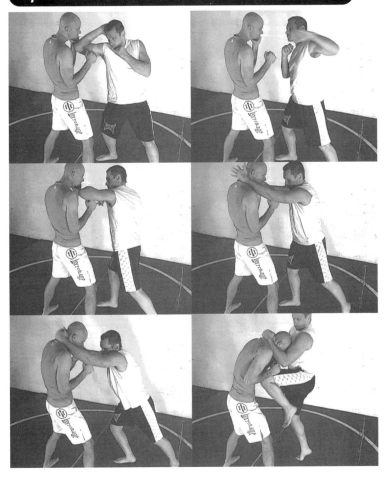

12. Kick Combinations
Two-Point Combos

Double rear kick thigh

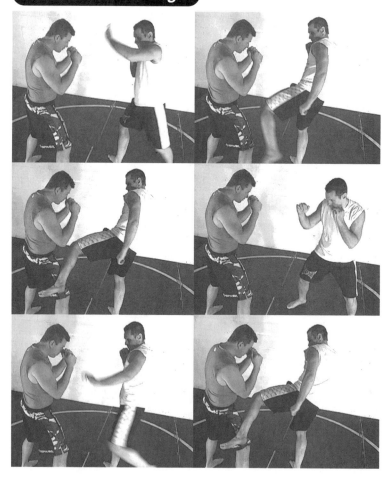

Double switch kick thigh

Double rear kick body

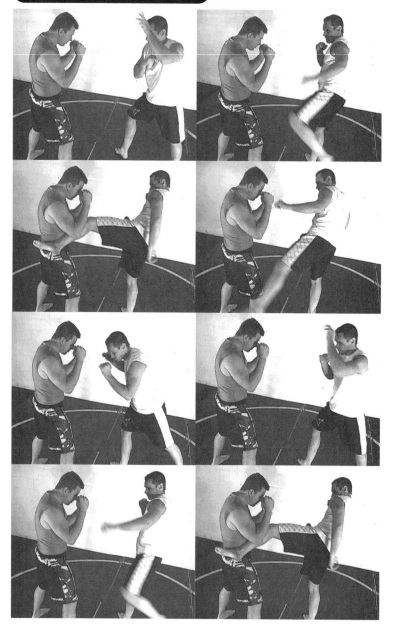

Double switch kick body

Double rear kick thigh / body

Now try it in reverse — rear kick body / thigh.

Double switch kick thigh / body

Reverse again for a switch kick body / thigh.

Rear kick thigh / Switch kick thigh

Also try switch kick thigh / rear kick thigh.

Rear kick body / Switch kick body

Flip this for a switch kick body / rear kick body.**

**More variations include
Rear kick body / Switch kick thigh
Switch kick body / Rear kick thigh
Rear kick thigh / Switch kick body
Switch kick thigh / Rear kick body

Jab kick / Rear kick thigh

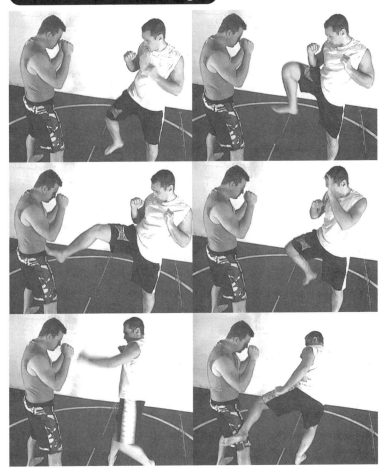

Inside kick / Rear kick thigh

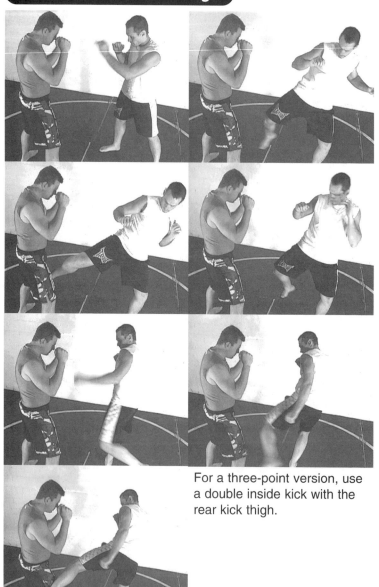

For a three-point version, use a double inside kick with the rear kick thigh.

13. Kick and Knee Combinations

Rear kick thigh / Lead skip knee

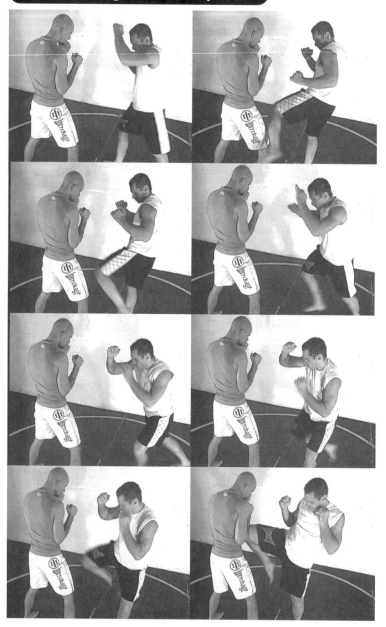

Rear straight knee / Switch kick thigh

Inside kick / Lead skip knee

Inside kick / Rear straight knee

Jab kick / Rear knee

Jab kick / Rear kick thigh / Lead skip knee

Striking to Entering

Striking to the clinch or striking to the takedown are far more successful ways to get to the grappling aspect of the game than free shooting (shooting without benefit of a strike setting up the entry). Strikes are ideal to bridge the gap between a straight kickboxing match and turning the fight into a true MMA bout. The following menus offer the highest percentage entries for striking to clinching/shooting.

You will notice that some shots (takedown attempts) are preceded by only one or two strikes. This is not a breaking of the combination rule. In striking to takedown combinations, the takedown itself is classed as part of the combination. We will divide this material into two broad menus: Striking to the Clinch (upper body grappling attack) and Striking to Takedown (lower body grappling attack). These lower body attacks can be any variety of doubles or singles, whatever the situation calls for.

I encourage you to learn to shoot off of any of the other combinations in any menu that does not specifically mention a takedown. The effortless blending between striking and clinching/shooting/grappling is what makes this game what it is.

14. Striking to Clinch
Two-Point Combos

Jab head to clinch

Lead hook head to clinch

Overhand to clinch

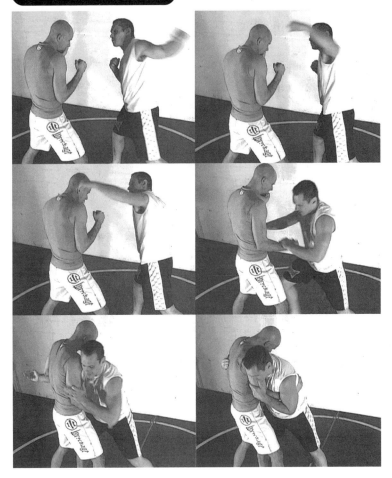

Lead muffle to clinch

A muffle is akin to a jab, but you throw the lead hand with an open palm attempting to "muffle" your opponent's lead hand to mute his counter striking. Follow the muffled hand inside to clinch.

Rear elbow to clinch

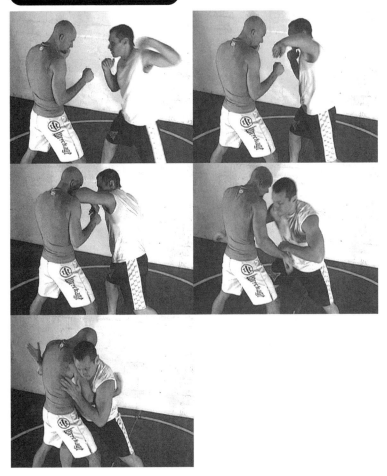

15. Striking to Clinch
Three-Point Combos

Jab head / Rear muffle to clinch

Lead hook head / Rear knee to clinch

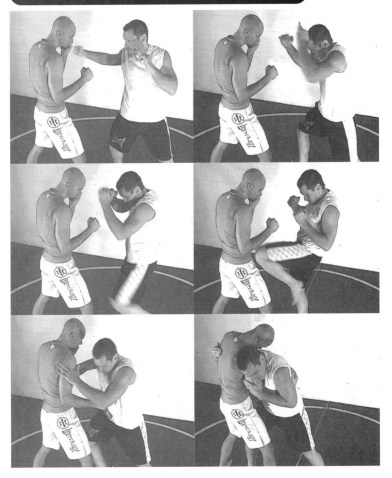

Jab head / Lead elbow to clinch

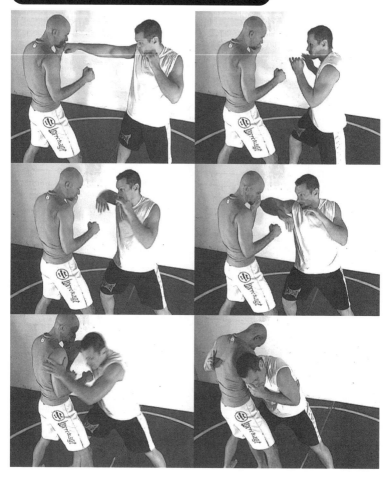

16. Striking to Takedown
Two-Point Combos

Jab head / Shoot

Cross head / Shoot

Overhand / Shoot

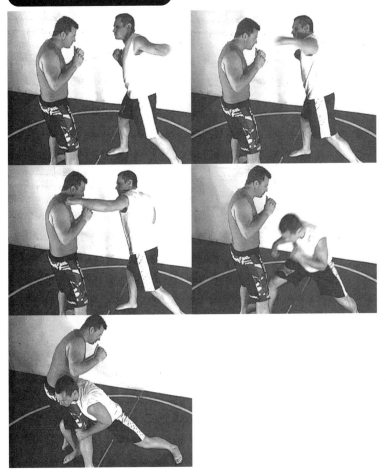

Lead uppercut / Shoot

Leg kick / Shoot

Jab kick / Shoot

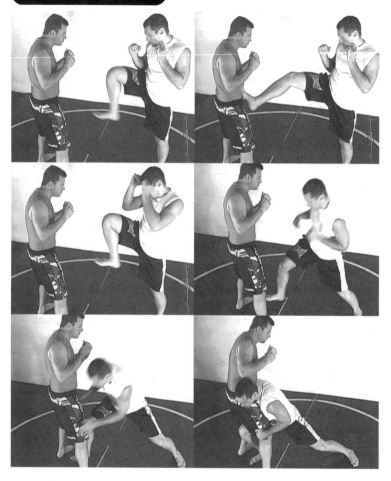

17. Striking to Takedown
Three-Point Combos

Double jab / Shoot

Jab head / Cross head / Shoot

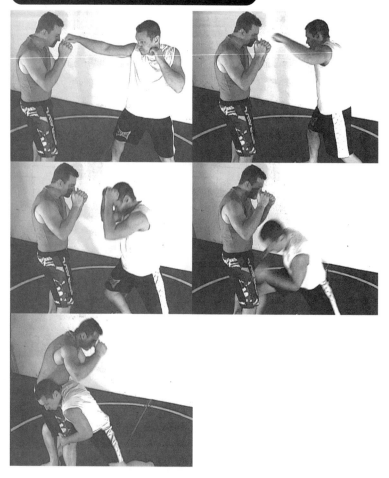

Jab head / Cross body / Shoot

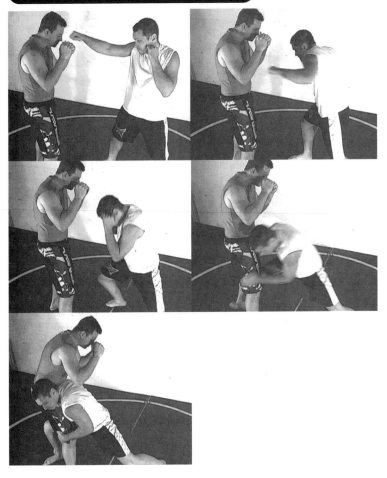

Cross head / Lead hook head / Shoot

Rear hook head / Lead hook head / Shoot

18. Chunking
Adding Combos Together

There it is. Over 175 of the highest yielding striking combinations culled from elite level MMA competition. All of them are arranged by the number or their constituent parts and the tools that comprise them for easy access. Let's assume for a moment that we all see merit in the Rule of 3's approach. With that assumption there might be one objection to the Rule of 3's strategy. And that is the predictability factor.

We may not be predictable as to what exactly the combination itself may be with 175-plus choices to cycle through. I don't think there is an opponent in the world with that sort of predictive power. But we can become very predictable in the "Oh, this guy always throws in threes" sense. That would be potentially problematic if it weren't for chunking.

Chunking is an inelegant term for how we compartmentalize information for easier recall. Let's use holding a phone number in our short term memory, for example. We hold the first three digits with no problem and then approach the last four digits with lots of silent repetition so we don't forget. Chunking as applied to striking combinations works in a similar manner. A two-point combination and a three-point combination bring us to a five pointer. Or we can add two three pointers for six-point combinations. With your system grooved for two- and three-point combinations, there will be little problem in reaching higher numbers by simply chunking any two (or more combinations) together.

To drill this concept I encourage you to experiment with chunking to find linked combinations that seem to flow best for you. But never lose sight of the fact that the sport (in it's current incarnation) seems to reward hewing closely to the Rule of 3's.

19. Counter Striking

Optimally, a manual on MMA combinations would contain both offensive and defensive combination work. As a matter of fact, that was the intention in the planning stage of this manual. But as the fight metrics added up, it became readily apparent that folding the two topics together would cause us to sacrifice page count to one or both topics. So we have emphasized offensive combination work and at another time will address defensive striking/counter striking in the detail it deserves.

No worries. Much of what you find between the covers of this book translates easily to counter striking work. To make this transition, you can take any combination and drill it in one of two ways (optimally both).

Defensive Counter Revolution Manner
Here you defend a strike from your partner and then launch your combination with the first strike originating from the side opposite the defending side. For example, you defend his lead hook with a rear cover (your rear hand) and then you begin your counter striking combination off a lead side weapon (your own hook or switch kick, for example).

Defensive Matched Revolution Manner
This means that you start your counter striking with a
tool on the same side as the defending side (using a jab
catch with the rear hand and then firing an overhand
with the same hand, as an example). This is obviously a
mirror image of the previous approach.

I think you'll find that working your way through the
combinations twice with the two described
approaches will build plenty of defensive counter
striking facility. If you feel that you need deeper work
on defensive response, I suggest that you pick up our
manual, *NHBF: Savage Strikes,* and use the defensive
chapters found there to better inform the counter
striking work.

Training Approaches
As we near the end, I offer six training drills to seat the
material and six attitudes color the drills (essentially
taking the drill set to 36 drills). The last combination
drill (Seven & Seven) will create some monstrous
striking endurance.

20. Six Drills

Drill 1: The Mirror

I heartily urge you to take advantage of mirror work when you first work a combination. Grab a spot in front of the glass and work a five-minute round slowly with an eye on watching for any holes or errors that can be fixed before adding any speed.

Work a second mirror round running at half speed watching for entropy and then one more round full speed. If you made it through all three rounds with something approaching perfection — good for you. Often, fundamental mirror work is given short shrift or ignored altogether. That's a pity since catching errors before they become "your style" is far easier than correcting erroneous style. Now it's time to hit something.

Drills 2 & 3: Heavy Bag/Shadow Striking Rotation

I'm a big fan of hitting the bag h-a-r-d as nothing builds striking power and specific striking conditioning like banging the bag. But I'm an even bigger fan of alternating rounds with full speed shadow striking. Where all-out bag work builds power and provides an easy target, full speed shadow work (not the controlled drills we did in front of the mirror) begins to build the facility needed for that "miss more than you hit" phenomenon we discussed earlier.

Isolating a heavy bag session at one time and then a shadow striking session at another does not provide the same "Aha" moment that moving straight from the bag to the air around you provides. It can be akin to wearing ankle weights all day and then taking them off.

Drill 4: Focus Pads / Thai Pads

Heavy bags are terrific, but they are solid, predictable targets. On the other hand, a good feeder (meaning an active feeder who will move, provide misses, hit back) is a whole new animal and the perfect next step to hone the combination of focus.

Drill 5: Give and Ye Shall Receive

This drill calls for you and your training partner/coach to gear up and fire the combinations back and forth in a tit-for-tat manner. Begin at light contact with each defending the strike and gradually increase in power and speed as you each build natural offensive and defensive fluidity. Again, approach these drills as alive as possible. Use good footwork, surprising movement, timing and so on. The elements of the drill may be predictable, but you do not have to be predictable in any other aspect.

Drill 6: Down & Out Drilling

Down & Out Drilling is putting it all together — striking, shooting, ground and pound, submissions, escapes, all of it. For a detailed look at Down & Out Drilling see our book in this series, *MMA Mastery: Flow Chain Drilling and Integrated O/D Training*.

21. Six Attitudes

Attitude is the mindset you bring to each combination. Ideally you will take each attitude described below and work it in each of the six aforementioned drills taking your drill varieties to 36 permutations.

I urge you not to discount the idea of attitude drilling. It goes a long way toward refining your own idiosyncratic style and also provides you with insight as to how other stylists approach the game. You should be better able to deal with what is not "natural" for you.

Attitude One: Lightweight
Bang through all the drills with an eye on maximum speed. Give no thought to power, loading up and/or putting strong hip into every strike. Just bang fast, fast, fast.

Attitude Two: Heavyweight
The inverse of the preceding attitude — bang hard with every shot. Speed is still nice, but do not let anything stand between you loading up and knocking every single one out of the park.

Attitude Three: Outsider
No matter your stature or reach, run through every combination as if you were six three with a reach of 80 inches. Loosen up your hooks, open those uppercuts, stay back on your straight shots, reach with those kicks. Keep a good distance between yourself and whatever surface you are striking.

Attitude Four: Insider

You are now five six with a reach of 60 inches, and you must stay inside. Get tight to your striking surface and stay there. Bring your head off only to fire the combination. Shorten the arc of all shots and chop instead of loop. Pop instead of reach.

Attitude Five: Counter Striker

Here you fire a combination only in response to an offensive stimulus. In the mirror or during shadow work you must envision the strike. On the bag your coach or partner can call "Now!" as opposed to allowing you to fire when you're set. With the pads you can fire only when the pads are flashed. Learn to be reactive as well as proactive.

Attitude Six: In & Out

This is a combination of attitudes three and four. Allow the first shot of your combination to be fired with the Outsider Attitude and then close immediately to finish with the Insider Attitude. As the last shot lands, get out fast.

22. Seven & Seven Drilling

The drill not the drink. The Seven & Seven I refer to is a heavy bag/banana bag drill set that will build striking combination endurance, adjust the balance between preferred striking modes (boxing versus kicking) and turn up some major heat on the conditioning.

Apart from drilling with a live partner, whether in a Down & Out or focus pad format, the most useful tool for solo striking training is the heavy bag. All too often the novice approaches the heavy bag with no plan beyond bang hard and look cool. That's not a bad plan, but the plan often deteriorates into throwing your pet punches and kicks with an ever decreasing cadence as the entropy of oxygen debt takes its toll.

Smart approaches to solo combat training gear involve tweaking a few elements to make sure that our practice is never rote and, if possible, pushing us to build new skills as well as conditioning. There are essentially two ways to tweak solo gear training. The first is the more common method of technique honing — using prescripted combinations and grooving them into your neuromuscular net. The second approach involves "gaming the gear."

Gaming the gear is imposing artificial guidelines, time limits and even an arbitrary scoring system. Seven & Seven belongs to this category. We'll use the Seven & Seven rules to highlight how the three principles (guidelines, time limits and scoring) can be used to keep motivation high when the body is less willing.

Seven & Seven Objectives
Conditioning and to force combinations across both major striking modes.

Seven & Seven Gear
● Heavy bag or banana bag (100 pounds minimum is ideal).

● Timer 1 — Set for two-minute rounds. (Low, huh? You'll see why in a moment.)

● Timer 2 — Set to chime every seven seconds.

● Appropriate striking gear (hand wraps, gloves, shin pads, whatever you deem necessary to bang the bag with safety).

● Training notebook to keep score.

● Partner — Not necessary, but ideal. The presence of another human to motivate and/or keep us honest is always a plus.

Seven & Seven Rules
● Start both timers.

● During the first seven-second interval, bang the bag with boxing combinations (elbows count).

● During the second seven seconds, bang the bag with lower body tools (kicks and/or knees).

● Alternate every seven seconds until the two-minute round is up.

Seven & Seven Scoring
Your score is the highest number of landed strikes inside each seven-second interval.

Example: If you land five punches in the first interval and three kicks in the next seven seconds, your punch/kick score is 5/3, but there are two catches …

Catch One
The scores are not cumulative. In other words, no adding up five punches plus three punches, etc.

Catch Two
You're only as good as your lowest score. Therefore if you land six punches per punch interval early in the round as well as four kicks/knees per interval early on, terrific. But if by the end your score drops to three punches and two kicks per interval, the lower score is always your final score no matter where it occurs in the two-minute round.

This scoring system keeps us motivated and is designed to teach you to give your all no matter where you are in the round. Ideally, you will have a training partner so that you can alternate rounds competing with one another for better scores. Even without a partner, the scoring system allows you to check progress. Simply record your score for that session (only record the lowest scores no matter what round they occurred in) and always strive to match or beat the score in your next session. Have fun!

Conclusion

We are at the end, the portion of the material that is either never read or read only once. For those who have stuck around this far, thanks. Please give serious thought to the Six Drills and the Six Attitudes. I think you'll find that these are just as important as the combinations themselves. As a matter of fact, I can say with some confidence that it is the drills and attitudes that will bring the combinations to their full potential rather than just rote repetition with no thought to altering the tone and timbre of the strikes.

I hope you enjoy the work. If you have any questions or would like further information on the subject, feel free to visit our Website at www.extremeselfprotection.com or contact us via e-mail at mark@extremeself-protection.com

Thanks! Train hard, train smart!

Mark Hatmaker

Resources

BEST CHOICES

First, please visit my Web site at
www.extremeselfprotection.com
You will find even more training
material as well as updates and
other resources.

Amazon.com

The place to browse for books such
as this one and other similar titles.

Paladin Press
www.paladin-press.com

Paladin carries many training
resources as well as some of my
videos, which allow you to see
much of what is covered in my
NHB books.

Ringside Boxing
www.ringside.com

Best choice for primo equipment.

Sherdog.com

Best resource for MMA news, event
results and NHB happenings.

Threat Response Solutions
www.trsdirect.com

They also offer many training
resources along with some of my
products.

Tracks Publishing
www.trackspublishing.com

They publish all the books in the
NHBF series and MMA series as
well as a few fine boxing titles.

www.humankinetics.com

Training and conditioning info.

www.matsmatsmats.com

Best resource for quality mats at
good prices.

Video instruction

Extreme Self-Protection
extremeselfprotection.com

Paladin Press
paladin-press.com

Threat Response Solutions
trsdirect.com

World Martial Arts
groundfighter.com

Events

IFC
ifc-usa.com

IVC
valetudo.com

King of the Cage
kingofthecage.com

Pancrase
so-net.ne.jp/pancrase

Pride
pridefc.com

The Ultimate Fighting
Championships
ufc.tv

Universal Combat Challenge
ucczone.ca/

Index

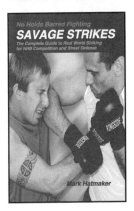

Boxing Mastery
Advance Techniques, Tactics and Strategies from the Sweet Science
Advanced boxing skills and ring generalship.
1-884654-21-5 / $12.95
900 photos

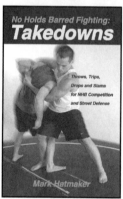

No Holds Barred Fighting:
Takedowns
Throws, Trips, Drops and Slams for NHB Competition and Street Defense
1-884654-25-8 / $12.95
850 photos

No Holds Barred Fighting:
The Clinch
Offensive and Defensive Concepts Inside NHB's Most Grueling Position
1-884654-27-4 / $12.95
750 photos

No Holds Barred Fighting:
The Ultimate Guide to Conditioning
Elite Exercises and Training for NHB
Competition and Total Fitness
1-884654-29-0 / $12.95
900 photos

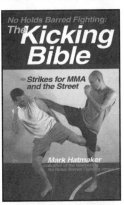

No Holds Barred Fighting:
The Kicking Bible
Strikes for MMA and the Street
1-884654-31-2 / $12.95
700 photos

No Second Chance:
A Reality-Based Guide to Self-Defense
How to avoid and survive an assault.
1-884654-32-0 / $12.95
500 photos

No Holds Barred Fighting:
The Book of Essential Submissions
How MMA champions gain their victories. A catalog of winning submissions.
1-884654-27-4 / $12.95
750 photos

MMA Mastery: Flow Chain Drilling
and Integrated O/D Training
to Submission Wrestling
Blends all aspects of the MMA fight game into devastating performances.
1-884654-38-x / $13.95
800 photos

MMA Mastery: Ground and Pound
A comprehensive go-to guide — how to win on the ground.
1-884654-39-8 / $13.95
650 photos

Mark Hatmaker is the bestselling author of the *No Holds Barred Fighting Series*, the *MMA Mastery Series*, *No Second Chance* and *Boxing Mastery*. He also has produced more than 40 instructional 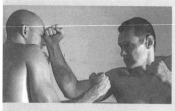 videos. His resume includes extensive experience in the combat arts including boxing, wrestling, Jiujitsu and Muay Thai.

He is a highly regarded coach of professional and amateur fighters, law enforcement officials and security personnel. Hatmaker founded Extreme Self Protection (ESP), a research body that compiles, analyzes and teaches the most effective Western combat methods known. ESP holds numerous seminars throughout the country each year including the prestigious Karate College/Martial Arts Universities in Radford, Virginia. He lives in Knoxville, Tennessee.

 www.extremeselfprotection.com
